‖‖‖ ‖‖ ‖‖‖‖ ‖‖‖ ‖‖‖‖‖ ‖‖ ‖‖‖
W9-BAI-386

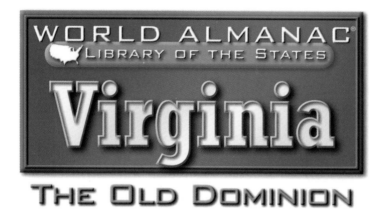

WORLD ALMANAC® LIBRARY OF THE STATES

Virginia

THE OLD DOMINION

by Pamela Pollack

Curriculum Consultant: Jean Craven,
Director of Instructional Support,
Albuquerque, NM, Public Schools

WORLD ALMANAC® LIBRARY

j975.5
pol

Please visit our web site at: **www.worldalmanaclibrary.com**
For a free color catalog describing World Almanac® Library's list of high-quality books
and multimedia programs, call 1-800-848-2928 or fax your request to (414) 332-3567.

Library of Congress Cataloging-in-Publication Data

Pollack, Pamela.
    Virginia, the Old Dominion / by Pamela Pollack.
       p. cm. — (World Almanac Library of the States)
    Includes bibliographical references and index.
    Summary: Illustrations and text present the history, geography, people, politics and
government, economy, and social life and customs of Virginia, which was first colonized
by the English in 1607.
    ISBN 0-8368-5125-0 (lib. bdg.)
    ISBN 0-8368-5293-1 (softcover)
    1. Virginia—Juvenile literature. [1. Virginia.] I. Title. II. Series.
F226.3.P65   2002
975.5—dc21   2001046993

This edition first published in 2002 by
World Almanac® Library
330 West Olive Street, Suite 100
Milwaukee, WI 53212 USA

This edition © 2002 by World Almanac® Library.

Design and Editorial: **Jack&Bill**/Bill SMITH STUDIO Inc.
Editors: Jackie Ball and Kristen Behrens
Art Directors: Ron Leighton and Jeffrey Rutzky
Photo Research and Buying: Christie Silver and Sean Livingstone
Design and Production: Maureen O'Connor and Jeffrey Rutzky
World Almanac® Library Editors: Patricia Lantier, Amy Stone, Valerie J. Weber,
Catherine Gardner, Carolyn Kott Washburne, Alan Wachtel, Monica Rausch
World Almanac® Library Production: Scott M. Krall, Eva Erato-Rudek, Tammy Gruenewald,
Katherine A. Goedheer

Photo credits: p. 5 © PhotoDisc; p. 6 (from top to bottom) © Corel, © Corel, © ArtToday;
p. 7 (top to bottom) © ArtToday, © PhotoSpin, © Painet; p. 9 © PhotoDisc; p. 10 © ArtToday;
p. 11 © Bettmann/CORBIS; p. 12 © Corel; p. 13 (top) © Corel, (bottom) © ArtToday; p. 14
© Library of Congress; p. 15 © William F. Campbell/TimePix; p. 17 © Corel; p. 18 © PhotoDisc;
p. 19 © Library of Congress; p. 20 (all) © Corel; p. 21 (from left to right) © Corel, © Painet,
© Corel; p. 23 © Corel; p. 24 © Dr. Pepper Museum; p. 26 (all) © PhotoDisc; p. 27 © Corel;
p. 29 © PhotoDisc; p. 30 courtesy of the General Assembly of Virginia; p. 31 (all) © Library of
Congress; p. 32 (from left to right) © Dover Publications, © Underwood & Underwood/CORBIS;
p. 33 © Will McIntyre/TimePix; p. 34–35 (all) © Corel; p. 36 © Library of Congress; p. 37
© Doug Pensinger/TimePix; p. 39 (top) © ArtToday, (bottom) © ArtToday; p. 40 (clockwise)
© PhotoDisc, © PhotoDisc, © PhotoDisc, © Library of Congress; p. 41 © Tony Triolo/TimePix;
p. 42–43 © Library of Congress; p. 44 (clockwise) © Artville, © PhotoDisc, © PhotoSpin;
p. 45 © Corel

All rights reserved. No part of this book may be reproduced, stored in a retrieval system,
or transmitted in any form or by any means, electronic, mechanical, photocopying, recording,
or otherwise, without the prior written permission of the copyright holder.

Printed in the United States of America

1 2 3 4 5 6 7 8 9 06 05 04 03 02

Virginia

Cradle of a Country

The story of Virginia is also the story of the United States. From its colonial beginnings as a British money-making venture sponsored by the Virginia Company of London, it became the birthplace of many leaders of the American Revolution and a key battleground in the Civil War. Virginia's history teaches us how we developed as a nation.

Eight presidents — the most from any one state — and some of the greatest statesmen the United States has ever produced were born here, forming ideas that would shape a nation. Virginia produced the first representative assembly in the New World, electing members to the House of Burgesses (now called the Virginia General Assembly) in 1619. Three Virginians — Thomas Jefferson, James Madison, and George Mason — were the architects of the Declaration of Independence, the Constitution, and the Bill of Rights, the three most important documents in U.S. government and law. George Washington, the nation's first president, was a Virginian. As commander-in-chief, Washington won the Revolutionary War's decisive battle at Yorktown, Virginia.

Virginia was at the epicenter of the Civil War, which took five hundred thousand lives — more than any other war in U.S. history — and put an end to slavery. Today Virginia is still at the forefront of the country's government and growth. While the battle for civil rights for all citizens was being waged throughout the states, Virginia struggled, too, and finally won; in 1990 L. Douglas Wilder was the first African-American governor elected in the United States. Virginia is now one of the fastest growing states, both in population and in its economy. Many federal government agencies have their offices in Virginia, and the federal government is one of the state's largest employers.

▶ Natural Bridge in the Blue Ridge Mountains. Thomas Jefferson bought this bridge and 157 surrounding acres for 20 shillings in 1774.

▶ Map of Virginia showing interstate highway system, as well as major cities and waterways.

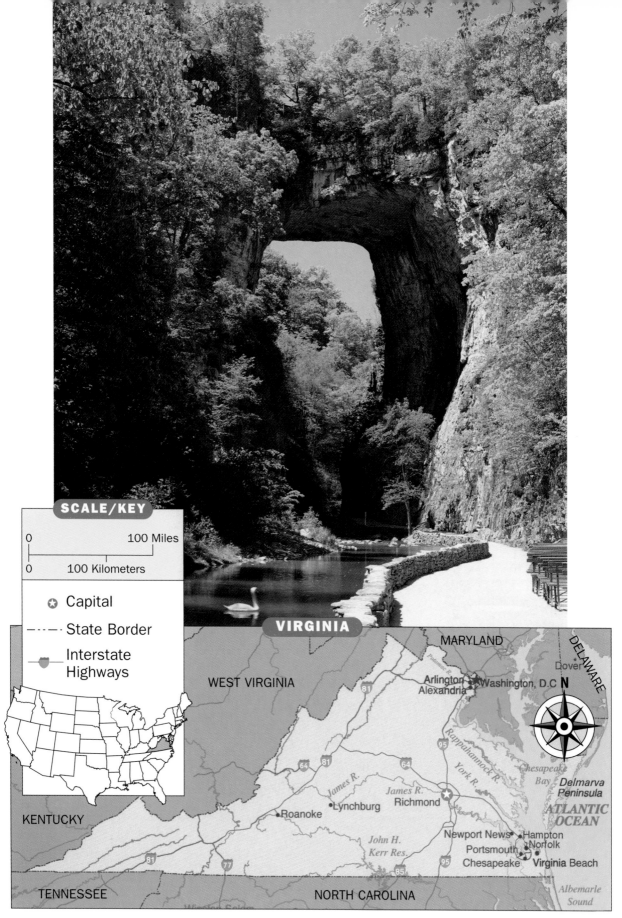

SCALE/KEY

0   100 Miles

0   100 Kilometers

⭐ Capital

—·—·— State Border

🛡 Interstate Highways

VIRGINIA

MARYLAND

DELAWARE

Dover

WEST VIRGINIA

Arlington   Washington, D.C

Alexandria

Potomac R.

81

Rappahannock R.

95

64

64

York R.

Chesapeake Bay

Delmarva Peninsula

James R.

81

James R.

Richmond ⭐

ATLANTIC OCEAN

KENTUCKY

Roanoke

Lynchburg

John H. Kerr Res.

Newport News

Hampton

Portsmouth

Norfolk

81

77

95

Chesapeake

Virginia Beach

85

TENNESSEE

NORTH CAROLINA

Albemarle Sound

N

Fast Facts

VIRGINIA (VA), The Old Dominion

Entered Union

June 25, 1788 (10th state)

Capital	Population
Richmond	197,790

Total Population

7,078,515 (12th most populous state)

Largest Cities	Population
Virginia Beach	425,527
Norfolk	234,403
Chesapeake	199,184
Richmond	197,790

Land Area

39,594 square miles (102,548 square kilometers) (37th largest state)

State Motto

"Sic Semper Tyrannis" — Latin for "Thus always to tyrants"

State Song

"Carry Me Back to Old Virginia" by James A. Bland — *As of today, Virginia has yet to find a replacement for "Carry Me Back to Old Virginia," which was officially retired by the General Assembly in 1997. The song, written by a black minstrel in the 1870s, depicts a slave's fond reminiscences for his days working under his master and offended African Americans and whites alike.*

State Dog

American fox hound — Fox hunting, an old Colonial tradition, is still popular today in Virginia's hunt country. In Leesburg there is even a Museum of Hounds and Hunting that is dedicated to the history of the sport in Virginia.

State Bird

Cardinal

State Fish

Brook trout — This member of the salmon family thrives in the mountain rivers and streams of Virginia.

State Insect

Tiger Swallowtail Butterfly — With yellow and black striped wings and a dark tail, it is one of the most commonly seen butterflies in the eastern United States.

State Flower

American dogwood blossom

State Tree

American dogwood

State Shell

Oyster shell — The Oyster and Maritime Museum in Chincoteague celebrates the importance of the seafood industry in Virginia from the 1600s to today.

State Beverage

Milk

State Folk Dance

Square Dance — *U.S. folk dance that originated in English country dance and French ballroom dance. It includes squares, clogging, line dances, and the Virginia reel among others.*

PLACES TO VISIT

Arlington National Cemetery *Arlington*
America's most famous cemetery, on a ridge overlooking the Potomac River, honors U.S. soldiers killed in battle from the time of the Revolutionary War to today.

Assateague Island *on the Eastern Shore of Virginia*
A wildlife refuge and a habitat for pony-sized wild horses. Every July there is an annual pony penning and swim, where the wild horses are rounded up on Assateague and swim across to reach Chincoteague Island.

The Appomattox Court House National Historical Park
It was in this village, at Appomattox Court House, that Robert E. Lee surrendered to Ulysses S. Grant in 1865, essentially ending the Civil War.
For other places and events, see p. 44

BIGGEST, BEST, AND MOST

- The Pentagon, the five-sided headquarters of the U.S. military establishment in Arlington, Virginia, is the United States's largest office building, with more than 6.5 million square feet (603,850 square meters) of space, 15 miles (24 kilometers) of corridors, and enough phone cable to wrap around the Earth three times.

- The Chesapeake Bay Bridge–Tunnel, considered one of the man-made wonders of the world, is 17 miles (27 km) long and runs over and under the mouth of Chesapeake Bay, between the Eastern Shore and Norfolk. From the middle of the bridge, it is almost impossible to see dry land.

STATE FIRSTS

- 1619 — The House of Burgesses was established, the first law-making body in America with elected representatives
- 1789 — Virginia's George Washington became first president of the United States
- 1981 — The United States's first test-tube baby was delivered at Norfolk General Hospital

The Gray Ghost

Confederate Major John Singleton Mosby was known as the Gray Ghost. *Gray* was for his uniform, and *ghost* was because he and his men carried out their raids on Union posts in Maryland and northern Virginia in a hit-and-run style, disappearing into the night like ghosts.

Brown's Box

In 1856 a Virginia slave named Henry Brown took a wild chance to escape to freedom. He got into a box with food and water and had himself mailed north to Philadelphia. When Brown stepped out of his box upon arrival, he was a free man.

▼ **The Appomattox Court House.**

The Origins of Liberty

> I know not what course others may take, but as for me,
> give me liberty, or give me death.
> — *Patrick Henry*

More than five thousand years ago, Native settlers probably immigrated across North America to inhabit the region that would become Virginia. These people began as nomadic hunters but gradually developed basic agriculture, cultivating crops of corn, squash, and beans.

By the 1600s the Native Americans were living in villages by rivers and on hillsides in a confederacy of thirty tribes under the leadership of Chief Wahunsonacock (known as Powhatan to the English) in 1607. They spoke dialects of the Algonquian language; they fished, hunted, farmed, and made jewelry from shells, pearls, and clay beads.

The Colony at Jamestown

Into this world sailed three ships bearing 105 Englishmen planning to start a colony and find their fortunes in gold and silver. The land was fertile with plenty of animals to hunt for food, but the English settlers were largely gentlemen adventurers with little idea of how to survive.

The fort they built at Jamestown — the first permanent English settlement in North America — was in a salt marsh, and there was little fresh water to drink. Disease ran rampant, and by the end of the first summer, almost half of the colonists were dead. With the exception of Captain John Smith, who had arrived a year later, few of the remaining colonists could provide food for themselves by hunting and fishing. They had not had time to plant crops.

John Smith

John Smith led expeditions to trade with the Native Americans for food and was captured and brought to Chief Powhatan. According to Smith he was saved from execution

Native Americans of Virginia
Appomatuck
Arrohateck
Kecougtan
Mattaponi
Nanticoke
Pamunkey
Powhatan Confederacy
Tauxent
Youghtamund

DID YOU KNOW?

Pocahontas's real name was Makatoa, and she may have "saved" John Smith's life during a traditional ceremony. Some historians believe Smith's life was never really in danger.

◀ This monument in Jamestown, the first permanent settlement in the original thirteen colonies, stands as a tribute to the United States.

when Powhatan's daughter, Pocahontas, intervened on his behalf. This led to a period of friendship between Powhatan and the colonists, which helped ease the hunger problem for a while. Finally a ship arrived from England bringing supplies. Under Smith's direction the colonists began to improve the settlement.

Smith was later wounded in a gunpowder explosion and returned to England to recover. The colonists' relationship with the Powhatan Confederacy fell apart, and famine followed in the winter of 1609–1610. It was called "the starving time." One colonist killed and ate his wife. A fellow

DID YOU KNOW?

Virginia was named for the Virginia Company (which had financed Jamestown's first settlers), which in turn was named for England's "Virgin Queen," Elizabeth I.

colonist wrote, ". . . hee was executed, as hee well deserved, now whether shee was better roasted, boyled, or carbonado'd, I know not . . ."

Saved by Tobacco

When John Smith left Jamestown in September 1609, about five hundred people were living there. By the spring of 1610 only sixty colonists were still alive. The survivors were planning to abandon the colony when they heard that three well-stocked English ships were on the way. One prominent newcomer was John Rolfe, who a few years later would create a type of tobacco that became wildly popular in England. The money raised by the crop helped support the colony. Not only did Rolfe develop a money-making crop but he also married Pocahontas, which pleased Powhatan and led to a peace pledge that would last eight years.

By 1619 the population had grown to almost twenty-two hundred. For the first time the colonists were allowed some self-government. They elected men to a law-making body called the House of Burgesses. In addition there was a governor appointed by the Virginia Company. Although the House of Burgesses' decisions could be overruled by this governor, it was still the first example of elected officials representing the will of the people in what would later become the United States.

Spitfire of the Revolution

In 1765 Patrick Henry, a member of the House of Burgesses, introduced seven resolutions that condemned Great Britain's tax laws. Many of the other Burgesses, who were wealthy from business dealings with England, considered Henry's proposals treasonous. As fellow Virginian Thomas Jefferson later said, the "ball of revolution" started rolling with Patrick Henry.

DID YOU KNOW?

Virginians claim that the first Thanksgiving in North America was held in Virginia in 1619.

◀ A depiction of the marriage ceremony between Pocahontas and John Rolfe.

That same year brought the arrival of mail-order brides, whose passages were paid for by their future husbands with 120 bags of tobacco. It also brought a Dutch trading ship carrying twenty slaves from Africa. At first these slaves were more like indentured servants and could earn their freedom after working for a number of years. By the late 1600s, however, the majority of the African Americans in Virginia were slaves.

British Rule Comes to Virginia

Virginia became a royal colony in 1624, when the Virginia Company's charter was revoked. Jamestown came under the direct rule of the British crown.

By the mid-1700s France was contesting English control of the Ohio Valley, leading to the French and Indian War (1754–1763). Many Native Americans fought with the French. The French were more interested in trade than colonizing, and Native Americans feared the further expansion of European settlements. Although little fighting took place in Virginia, it played a large role in providing men and supplies for the British war effort. A twenty-one-year-old Virginian named George Washington led troops against the French. He distinguished himself in battle and later became a major figure in the formation of the United States.

Britain had large debts after the French and Indian War and decided that the colonies in North America should pay their share. Starting in 1764 Great Britain began taxing the colonists, who resented being taxed without having any say in the British Parliament. "Taxation without representation is tyranny," they said. In addition, after having lived in the colonies for several generations, many no longer considered themselves English and did not like the idea of being ruled by a faraway nation most had never seen.

Bacon's Rebellion

The first serious conflict between the Virginians and their British rulers came in 1676 when Nathaniel Bacon, a tobacco plantation owner, led an attack against a Powhatan village in retaliation for previous Indian attacks. The British governor, William Berkeley, had refused to help the colonists in their fight with Native Americans, and after Bacon attacked the Native Americans, Berkeley labeled him a traitor. That summer Bacon and his followers fought the governor's forces, forcing Berkeley to flee, and burned Jamestown. Bacon's Rebellion fell apart when he became sick and died that October. Berkeley executed twenty of the Rebellion's leaders, but this was just the beginning of a deepening rift between the colonists and the mother country.

Stirrings of Revolution

In 1774 Britain's royal governor closed the House of Burgesses, and Patrick Henry, a Virginia lawyer and member of the House of Burgesses, called for a complete break with England. At a meeting in a Richmond church, he proclaimed, "Gentlemen may cry, peace, peace — but there is no peace . . . is life so dear, or peace so sweet, as to be purchased at the price of chains and slavery . . . I know not what course others may take, but as for me, give me liberty or give me death!"

Henry's words inspired Virginians to take up arms to defend their colony. Patriots in the other twelve colonies also began planning to arm themselves against the British. Shortly thereafter the Revolutionary War began. George Washington was chosen as commander in chief of the Continental Army and went to Boston to begin training the troops. Virginian Thomas Jefferson was asked to explain the colonists' position to England's King George. His Declaration of Independence was adopted by the Continental Congress on July 4, 1776. In it he described the rebelling colonists as the "united States of America."

Nat Turner's Rebellion

In 1831 a slave preacher named Nat Turner led a rebellion in South Hampton County, killing fifty-eight whites, mostly women and children. Turner and his followers were hanged, and at least a hundred innocent slaves were also murdered by angry whites. By the mid-1800s slavery became illegal in the industrialized North.

▼ This 1820 painting by Connecticut painter John Trumbull depicts the surrender of General Cornwallis's troops to General Washington.

Virginia became a state in June 1776, with a Bill of Rights written for its Constitution by George Mason. It would later become the tenth state to join the United States under the 1787 U.S. Constitution. Mason's Bill of Rights was intended to protect the rights and freedoms of all Virginians, including the freedoms of speech and religion. The final battle of the revolution was won in Yorktown, Virginia, on October 19, 1781. British General Charles Cornwallis surrendered to George Washington and his army. The battle for independence was won, and a new set of governing laws was needed. Virginia's James Madison, the "father of the Constitution," guided its creation with other U.S. leaders. The U.S. Constitution (1787) would be the framework for the new country's government. George Mason's Bill of Rights was used as the basis for the first ten constitutional amendments (1791).

▲ Moore House was the site of the signing of the final articles of surrender.

The Growing Pains of a New Nation

George Washington, the hero of the revolution, was elected to serve as first president of the United States. The third, fourth, and fifth presidents — Thomas Jefferson, James Madison, and James Monroe — were also Virginians.

While the soil of Virginia seemed to produce great statesmen, it could not grow much else any longer, especially in the east. Tobacco farming had exhausted the land. Some Virginians turned to trading slaves, who were sold to plantation owners in other southern states.

Many northerners wanted the South to outlaw slavery as well. Abraham Lincoln was elected president in 1860 on a platform that called for its abolition. Many southern states began to secede from the Union, forming the Confederate States of America. In 1861 the Civil War began when the Confederates fired on a Union fort. When Lincoln ordered the Virginia militia to fight for the northern side, Virginia left the Union, refusing to fight against its fellow Southerners. Richmond became the capital of the Confederacy, with Virginian General Robert E. Lee as Confederate military leader. The pro-Union northwestern part of the state split off to form West Virginia in 1863.

▲ Gentleman farmer and first U.S. president George Washington.

The Civil War and Its Aftermath

As home to the Confederate capital and border state to Washington, D.C., the Union capital, Virginia experienced more battles than any other state. Almost twenty-two hundred of the war's four thousand battles were fought in Virginia, and the first battle between two ironclad ships, the *Virginia (Merrimack)* and the *Monitor*, took place in the waters off Hampton Roads. After four years of the costliest war in U.S. history, the Confederacy was defeated. On April 9, 1865, General Robert E. Lee surrendered to Union General Ulysses S. Grant at Appomattox. Virginia was readmitted to the union in 1870, but the state was devastated. Richmond and other major cities were in ruins, Virginia's currency was worthless, and much of the work-force had been wounded or killed in battle.

The 350,000 slaves were now free, but most were homeless and jobless, or else became sharecroppers working white-owned land for a tiny percentage of the crop. At the end of the war, Congress had created an agency to help freed slaves, called the Freedmen's Bureau. It only lasted for seven years but did help to open several schools for African Americans. Booker T. Washington was the most famous graduate of the Hampton Normal and Industrial Institute. He started the Tuskegee Institute in Alabama in 1881.

By the turn of the century, the small gains African Americans had achieved began to disappear. Legal segregation began in 1900 when the state passed a law

DID YOU KNOW?

Thomas Jefferson was the first person to use the name the United States of America.

DID YOU KNOW?

The battle between the two ironclads, the U.S.S. *Monitor* and the C.S.S. *Virginia,* lasted four hours and ended with neither ship damaged and both sides claiming victory.

▼ **Photographer Timothy H. O'Brien took this picture of Union soldiers at Appomattox Court House in April 1865.**

that required African Americans and whites to sit in separate railroad cars. Separate schools for blacks and whites were also established, and poll taxes and discriminatory tests made it almost impossible for African Americans to vote or participate in Virginia politics. Although slave owner Thomas Jefferson had written about all men being created equal, it would take years until his words held any meaning for African-American Virginians.

A Gradual Recovery

As the twentieth century progressed, Virginia slowly began to recover, developing industry and becoming less dependent on tobacco crops. A Virginian was again elected to the White House.
— Woodrow Wilson, served two terms as president, from 1913–1921

▲ In 1990 L. Douglas Wilder became the first African American to be elected governor in the United States.

The economy was stimulated by the two world wars, as money and workers poured into Virginia's shipyards and naval bases. In the meantime African Americans had been living under statewide segregation, many deciding to leave Virginia to find better lives. In 1954, in the *Brown v. Board of Education* decision, the Supreme Court declared segregation "inherently unequal, and therefore illegal." Virginians resisted this decision, and the Virginia General Assembly voted to withhold state funds from any integrated schools. By 1958 many integrated schools had closed. Although in 1959 Governor Lindsay Almond of Virginia was forced by the federal courts to accept integration, schools in Prince Edward County stayed closed until 1964. In 1964 and 1965 Federal civil-rights laws and the Twenty-fourth Amendment to the Constitution, barring poll taxes, helped minorities gain their full legal rights.

In the last half of the twentieth century, Virginia has undergone an economic and technological upsurge, leading to an incredible population explosion. In 1990 L. Douglas Wilder became governor of Virginia, the first African-American governor elected in the United States. By the year 2000 Virginia's population had passed the seven million mark. Virginia went from an impoverished, insulated state to a financial, manufacturing, and agricultural powerhouse.

September 11, 2001

The Pentagon, located in Arlington, is the headquarters of the U.S. armed forces. It was one target of a series of terrorist attacks that struck the United States on September 11, 2001. One of four passenger planes hijacked that day was deliberately crashed into the building, killing 125 people in the building, as well as the 58 passengers and the 6-person flight crew aboard the plane. The casualty rate within the Pentagon was lower than it might have been as the plane hit a section of the building under renovation.

From the Farm to the City

> Family trees that remember your grandfather's name.
>
> — *Stephen Vincent Benet*, John Brown's Body

Who Virginians Are

Since Virginia began as a colony in 1607, most of the population has been of Anglo-Saxon descent. Virginia didn't attract the immigrants who flocked to the industrial cities of the North at the turn of the twentieth century. Today, out of a population of more than 7 million, 72.3 percent are white. The first settlers in Jamestown belonged to the Anglican church. Later immigrants in the colonial period were Lutherans from Germany, Baptists from Wales, as well as English Quakers.

By 1700 the population had reached seventy thousand, of which 9 percent were slaves. Fifty years later the African-American population had risen to 40 percent. By the Revolutionary War, Virginia had a population of 550,000, and about 50 percent were African American. After slavery was ended many left Virginia for more favorable economic conditions, and today only 19.6 percent of the population is

Age Distribution in Virginia

0–4	461,982
5–19	991,039
20–24	484,065
25–44	2,718,229
45–64	1,630,867
65 and over	792,333

DID YOU KNOW?

The population of Virginia is 49 percent male and 51 percent female.

Patterns of Immigration

The total number of people who immigrated to Virginia in 1998 was 15,686. Of that number, the largest immigrant groups were from El Salvador (9%), Philippines (5.8%), and India (5.8%).

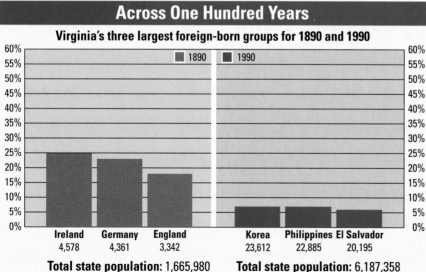

Across One Hundred Years

Virginia's three largest foreign-born groups for 1890 and 1990

■ 1890   ■ 1990

Ireland	Germany	England	Korea	Philippines	El Salvador
4,578	4,361	3,342	23,612	22,885	20,195

Total state population: 1,665,980
Total foreign-born: 18,374 (1%)

Total state population: 6,187,358
Total foreign-born: 311,809 (5%)

African American. Today the African-American population lives mostly in the Piedmont and coastal area. Central Richmond County is over 30 percent and Charles City County is over 50 percent African American.

▲ A Civil War-era re-enactment on stage in Lexington

Where Virginians Live

At the beginning of the twentieth century, only 15 percent of Virginians lived in cities. Today, however, the population is

Heritage and Background, Virginia   Year 2000

▶ Here's a look at the racial backgrounds of Virginians today. Virginia ranks eleventh among all U.S. states with regard to African Americans as a percentage of the population.

Total population 7,078,515

White
5,120,110
72.3%

Native Hawaiian and other Pacific Islander
3,946
0.1%

American Indian and Alaska Native
21,172
0.3%

Some other race
138,900
2.0%

Two or more races
143,069
2.0%

Asian
261,025
3.7%

Black or African American
1,390,293
19.6%

Note: 4.7% (329,540) of the Virginia population identify themselves as **Hispanic** or **Latino,** a cultural designation that crosses racial lines. Hispanics and Latinos are counted in this category and the racial category of their choice.

mostly urban. Nearly 75 percent of Virginia's population lives in the metropolitan corridor that stretches along the East Coast. Over the last few decades, Virginia's population growth has been higher than the rest of the nation's. As cities spread outward urban sprawl is becoming a problem. The most pronounced sprawl areas are in the Beltway (the area around Washington, D.C.) and in the Hampton Roads/Tidewater regions.

Despite racial inequalities of the past, different racial groups get along fairly well, although occasionally problems do arise. For example Martin Luther King, Jr., Day was designated Lee-Jackson-King Day, because Civil War generals Robert E. Lee and Stonewall Jackson, as well as King, were all born in January. Many Virginians felt it was inappropriate to combine the celebration of a civil rights leader with two men who fought to uphold slavery. A statue of African-American tennis champion Arthur Ashe, erected in 1996, also caused controversy. It was placed on Richmond's Monument

Just Say No

Virginians have been united in their state pride in two instances: They refused to allow Wal-Mart to build over George Washington's boyhood farm and successfully opposed Disney's plans for Disney's America, a history-themed amusement park.

Educational Levels of Virginia Workers	
Less than 9th grade	443,668
9th to 12th grade, no diploma	543,535
High school graduate, including equivalency	2,987,611
Some college, no degree or associate degree	955,518
Bachelor's degree	612,679
Graduate or professional degree	360,215

▼ The skyline of Richmond, Virginia's capital.

Avenue, which until then had been dedicated to those who fought for the Confederacy.

Religion

A majority of Virginians are Protestant. More than one-third belong to Baptist churches. Protestant Virginians also belong to Methodist, Episcopalian, and Presbyterian churches. Among the roughly 20 percent who are not Protestant, 7.4 percent are Catholic, 0.4 percent are Buddhist, and 0.2 percent are Muslim. About 0.6 percent of Virginians are agnostic, neither believing nor disbelieving in God. Virginia also has a small but growing Jewish population of about 1.1 percent. Hampton Roads has one of the country's fastest-growing Jewish communities. Richmond has one of the largest Jewish populations of any city its size in the country and two museums celebrating Richmond's Jewish heritage, including the Virginia Holocaust Museum, which pays tribute to those whose lives were forever changed by the Holocaust.

▲ General Robert E. Lee as photographed by Julian Vannerson in 1863.

Education

Public education in the southern states lagged behind that in the North in the early years of the nation. In the North life was centered on villages, and in the South, on plantations where the population was spread out over large expanses of land. The idea of education for all was not popular, a leftover of upper-class English attitudes. Public schools were not widely established in Virginia until 1846, although in 1642 poor children over the age of six began to receive religious instruction, as well as training in a trade, at a workhouse in James City. Other southern states followed Virginia's lead.

Higher education in Virginia began in 1693, when William and Mary College was founded. Initially intended to train men to be Anglican ministers, its mission was changed by Thomas Jefferson, who instituted the teaching of economics, law, mathematics, medicine, physics, and politics, among other things. Today Virginia has the eleventh largest system of higher education in the United States. The state is home to forty-eight accredited, four-year colleges and universities and four two-year community colleges, including the Virginia Community College System with its twenty-three locations.

Tidal Plains and Mountain Ranges

> Equal to the promised land in fertility, and far superior to it for beauty.
>
> — *Washington Irving's description of Virginia, circa 1830*

Virginia's mainland is in the rough shape of a triangle. There is one part of Virginia unconnected to the rest of the state — the Eastern Shore. It is part of a peninsula that extends down from Maryland between Chesapeake Bay and the Atlantic.

Throughout the seasons Virginia's climate remains relatively warm. Springs are mild, but summers tend to be hot, with high humidity making it seem even hotter. Autumns are cool but not cold, and temperatures rarely go below 32°F (0°C) in winter. Up to 10 inches (25 centimeters) of snow fall along the coast every year, while the mountains receive about 2 feet (.6 meters).

From sea level at the eastern coast, the land rises over 1 mile (1.6 kilometers) high in the mountains of the southwest, with the highest point being Mt. Rogers at 5,729 feet (1,746 m) above sea level. The three largest regions are the Tidewater or Coastal Plain; the Piedmont, the midsection of Virginia; and the mountainous area to the west.

The Tidewater

The Tidewater has a vast network of marshes, creeks, and rivers that open into estuaries. Estuaries form where salt

DID YOU KNOW?

The Blue Ridge Mountains are part of the Appalachian Mountain chain. The Blue Ridge Mountains extend from Virginia down through North Carolina.

▼ *From left to right:* **The Civil War battlefield at Manassas, now covered with grass; spring along the Blue Ridge Parkway; farmland in Madison County; the Shenandoah Caverns; the Shenandoah River; Virginia Beach.**

and freshwater meet, and the depth of the water ebbs and flows with the ocean's tides. Groves of hardwood trees lead into flooded forests of bald cypresses and black gums. These flooded forests largely have gone untouched for hundreds of years. The Great Dismal Swamp, which stretches south to North Carolina, is the biggest swamp in the Tidewater.

The Eastern Shore, Virginia's part of the Delmarva (Delaware-Maryland-Virginia) Peninsula, is famous for its wildlife. Assateague Island is a national seashore and wildlife refuge, home to more than 250 species of birds, including snow geese, herons, falcons, bald eagles, and pelicans. Sea turtles, dolphins, and whales are often seen off the coast. Chincoteague Island is famous for its salt oysters and home to the world's only oyster museum.

Chesapeake Bay

The largest inlet on the Atlantic coastal plane, Chesapeake Bay, is 120 miles (193 km) long and between 3 and 25 miles (4.8 to 40 km) wide. The bay was once home to a rich assortment of marine life, but pollution in the twentieth century has drastically reduced populations of fish and birds. Recently conservation efforts have had success in bringing life back to the bay.

Rivers and Wetlands

Of Virginia's more than one million acres of wetlands, the most common are swamps. Since the 1780s farmers, builders, and others have drained and/or filled in nearly half of the state's wetlands. Swamps serve as homes to complicated ecosystems including fish, reptiles, birds, and small mammals. They also serve to improve water quality in larger bodies of water, prevent floods, and control erosion of shorelines. There is no easy way to identify wetlands, as areas that are dry in some parts of the year may actually

DID YOU KNOW?

One of Virginia's largest lakes is man-made. Smith Mountain Lake was formed when the Blackwater and Roanoke Rivers were dammed in 1966 to create hydroelectric power for the region. The lake is high up in the Blue Ridge Mountains, and, when full, the water level is 795 feet (242 meters) above sea level.

Drain Dismal Swamp?

George Washington once planned to drain the Great Dismal Swamp. At the time swamps were considered a waste of what might be good farmland. Although his Great Dismal Swamp Land Company succeeded in digging several canals in the area, the swamp was finally too much for them, and all plans for drainage had to be abandoned.

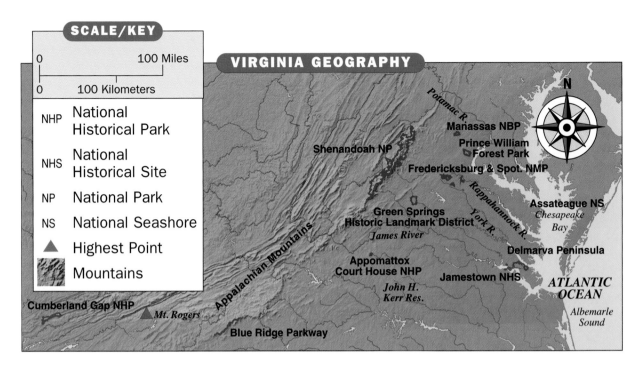

SCALE/KEY

NHP	National Historical Park
NHS	National Historical Site
NP	National Park
NS	National Seashore
▲	Highest Point
	Mountains

be submerged under water at other times. An area may be designated wetlands based on the types of plants, soil, or water found there.

Rivers have always been important in Virginia and have been used as highways since the earliest settlement of the area. Rivers such as the Rappahannock and the James, as well as many tributaries, made it possible for early European settlers to transport agricultural goods such as tobacco to the international ports on the Atlantic.

The Potomac River forms the northern border between Virginia and Maryland, running 383 miles (616 km) from its origin in the Appalachian Mountains through Washington, D.C., and emptying into the Chesapeake Bay. Residents of the nation's capital take 80 percent of their drinking water from the Potomac. The 340 mile (547 km) James River is crossed at Newport News by a bridge that is 4.5 miles (7 km) long.

The Piedmont

West from the Tidewater are the rolling hills of the Piedmont, which makes up the middle third of Virginia. Here, the sandy soil of the Tidewater changes to the central plain's harder metamorphic rock. Humans have had more impact on the Piedmont than on any other part of the state, turning much of the gently forested slopes into pastures, ponds, and pavement. Oaks are the most common trees left

Virginia Rivers

James
340 miles (547 km)

Potomac
285 miles (459 km)

Roanoke
45 miles (73 km)

New River
39 miles (63 km)

York
26 miles (41.8 km)

DID YOU KNOW?

The state flower is not really a flower but the blossom of the state tree, the dogwood tree.

High Point

Mt. Rogers
5,729 feet (1,746 m) above sea level

in the Piedmont, with maples, cypresses, and black gum trees lining the rivers. South of the James River, pine forests can be found. There remains an abundance of wildlife, including deer, raccoons, squirrels, and opossums. In the artificial lakes and on riverbanks, muskrats, beavers, and kingfishers can be found. The Piedmont is also home to box turtles and bullfrogs.

The Mountains

Between the Blue Ridge Mountains of the east and the Allegheny Mountains of the Appalachian range in the west lies the Shenandoah River Valley. The forests of the mountainous west include twenty-six species of trees, from hemlocks to tulip. The state tree — the American dogwood — blossoms in spring. The most common animals in the mountains are foxes, raccoons, rabbits, chipmunks, and skunks. White-tailed deer graze in Shenandoah National Park. Buzzards with a 6-foot (1.8-m) wingspan are a common sight, as are ravens and wild turkeys.

At many places near the Blue Ridge are scenic caves and caverns, including the Skyline Caverns at Front Royal to the north and the Luray Caverns to the west of Shenandoah National Park. The warm and hot springs that flow through Warm Spring Valley were discovered by Native Americans long before Europeans crossed the Blue Ridge.

In the extreme southwest corner of Virginia is Cumberland Gap, a natural pass through the Appalachian Mountains where Virginia, Tennessee, and Kentucky meet. The people who settled the lands west of Virginia passed through the Cumberland Gap. In the 1770s more than three hundred thousand people followed Daniel Boone through the gap to Kentucky. At that time it was the only way they could get wagons through the mountains.

Average January temperature
Richmond: 45°F (7°C) Virginia Beach: 47°F (8°C)

Average July temperature
Richmond: 88°F (31°C) Virginia Beach: 86°F (30°C)

Average yearly rainfall
Shenandoah Valley: 33 inches (83 cm) Southwestern mountains: more than 60 inches (152 cm)

Average yearly snowfall
20 inches (50 cm)

▼ A meadow of wildflowers in central Virginia.

From Tobacco to Technology

> He that will not worke shall not eat.
> — *Captain John Smith*

Until the dawn of the twentieth century, Virginia's economy primarily depended on agriculture. Today the majority of Virginia's revenue comes from shipbuilding, tobacco processing, and light industry, which includes chemicals, clothing, machinery, wood products, and food. While still significant, agriculture, along with the coastal fishing industry, are two of the smallest revenue producers in Virginia.

Shipbuilding and Shipping

Newport News Shipbuilding and Drydock Company in the Hampton Roads area is the world's largest privately owned shipyard, employing one-tenth of the population of Newport News. In nearby Norfolk is the world's largest naval facility, the Norfolk Naval Base. One-third of the workers in the Hampton Roads area work for the U.S. Department of Defense or private defense contractors. Hampton Roads is also the world's largest coal-shipping port.

Tobacco and Industry

Richmond, the state's capital, has always been one of Virginia's most important commercial hubs. More than a dozen Fortune 500 companies make their metals there, including one of the world's largest — Reynolds — which introduced aluminum foil to the world in 1947. Tobacco giant Philip Morris is the city's largest private employer. Tobacco, always lucrative, has also been the subject of a long-standing controversy. Once called "the esteemed weed," we know today that England's King James, an early nonsmoker in the 1600s, was right when he called the smoke of the tobacco plant "the horrible Stigian smoke of the pit that is bottomless . . ."

The Soda State

Virginians claim that two famous U.S. soft drinks, Mountain Dew (original slogan: Yahoo, Mountain Dew!) and Dr. Pepper, were both created near Marion in southwest Virginia. Pharmacist Dr. Charles Pepper's soda formula was supposedly stolen by a young assistant who ran away with one of Dr. Pepper's daughters.

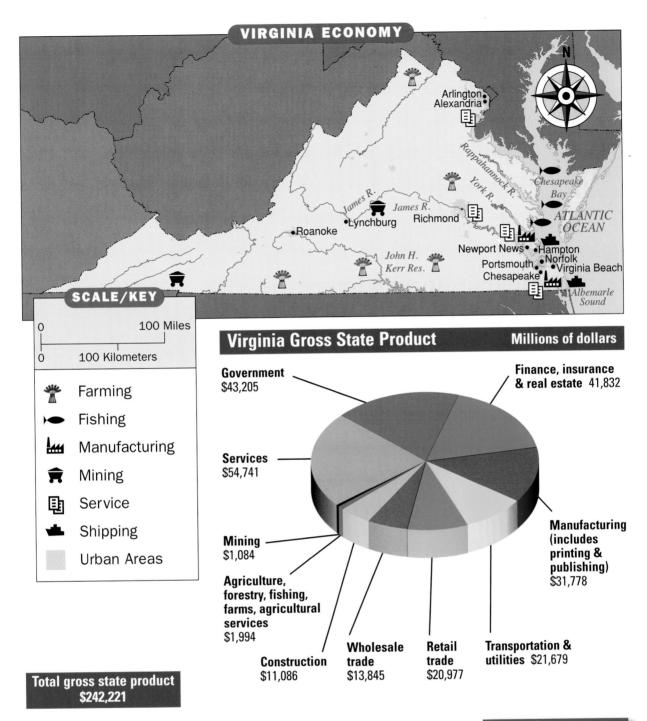

VIRGINIA ECONOMY

SCALE/KEY

0 — 100 Miles

0 — 100 Kilometers

- 🌾 Farming
- 🐟 Fishing
- 🏭 Manufacturing
- ⛏ Mining
- 📑 Service
- ⛴ Shipping
- ▫ Urban Areas

Virginia Gross State Product — Millions of dollars

- **Government** $43,205
- **Finance, insurance & real estate** 41,832
- **Services** $54,741
- **Manufacturing (includes printing & publishing)** $31,778
- **Mining** $1,084
- **Agriculture, forestry, fishing, farms, agricultural services** $1,994
- **Construction** $11,086
- **Wholesale trade** $13,845
- **Retail trade** $20,977
- **Transportation & utilities** $21,679

Total gross state product $242,221

Government and High-Tech

The largest concentration of government workers in Virginia can be found in the north, primarily in Arlington, home to the Pentagon, which alone employs almost twenty-four thousand government workers. Another large government employer is the Marine Corps Base in Quantico. Many Virginians commute to work in federal offices in Washington, D.C.

A boom of high-tech computer and communications

DID YOU KNOW?

Virginia was the first place in the United States to grow a peanut crop.

industries and the arrival of major corporate headquarters have added to northern Virginia's thriving economy. In recent years, the manufacturers of Richmond have been joined by high finance and high-tech concerns.

Coal Mining

At the turn of the twentieth century, coal mining took off when newly built railroads finally made it possible to transport coal to fuel ships and factories from the hills of southwest Virginia. In the 1920s coal mined there was used to manufacture steel. The industry declined after World War II, when oil and natural gas became the fuels of choice. The oil crisis of the 1970s brought back demand for a while, but the coal cities in southwestern Virginia today struggle to find new avenues of prosperity.

Agriculture

On Virginia's Eastern Shore, agriculture is the economic mainstay. Crops include potatoes, soybeans, and peanuts. Hogs are raised west of Norfolk and are made into the world-famous Smithfield hams.

Winchester in the Shenandoah River Valley is the largest city in Virginia's apple heartland of Frederick and Clark Counties and produces cider vinegar, apple butter,

Top Employers (of workers age sixteen and over)
Services 32%
Federal, state, . . .21% and local government (including military)
Wholesale and . .19% retail trade
Manufacturing . . .15% (food processing, textiles, electronic and electrical equipment)
Transportation, . .6.6% communications, and utilities
Agriculture, ...2.0% forestry, and fisheries

▼ *From left to right:* Workers watch as coal is mined; the shipyard in Norfolk.

and applesauce. Over half of the yearly crop, which can reach as high as 300 million pounds (136,080,000 kg) of apples, is sold fresh across the country.

Rockingham County in the Shenandoah Valley is number one in Virginia in the production of beef, dairy products, and poultry. It's also the second largest turkey producer in the country.

Coastal Fishing Industry

Beginning in 1996 Chesapeake Bay fishermen began experiencing health problems, and dead fish turned up by the thousands. It was discovered that a normally harmless bacteria had been turned toxic by chicken manure, which was used as fertilizer in local pastures. Runoff from the fields ended up in the bay. Seafood sales plummeted, and the industry has yet to fully recover. Conservationists are working to make the Chesapeake Bay area ecologically sound again. Today the main catches there are oysters, crabs, scallops, and clams as well as the inedible fish menhaden, which is used to make oil and fertilizer.

Tourism

Tourism is a gold mine for Virginia. Its hottest spot is the city of Virginia Beach, where tourism is the number one industry. The state also has twenty-six state parks, nine major lakes, a national seashore, and an abundance of wildlife refuges. Virginia also boasts a great number of historic sites, including famous battlefields and the homes of several presidents, such as Mount Vernon, the home of George Washington, and Monticello, Thomas Jefferson's home. Colonial Williamsburg, a restoration of Virginia's capital at the time of the American Revolution, is a major tourist attraction. There are also natural wonders to visit such as the Luray Caverns.

▲ The U.S. Congress agreed in 1926 that the Shenandoah National Park should be created but refused federal money to acquire land. Between that time and 1935, state money and private donations were used to acquire the land.

DID YOU KNOW?

Norfolk, Virginia, is the home base for the U.S. Navy's Atlantic Fleet.

Made in Virginia

Leading farm products and crops
Broilers (chickens)
Cattle
Dairy products
Tobacco

Other products
Textiles
Transportation equipment
Electric and electronic equipment
Processed food
Chemicals

International Airports		
Airport	Location	Passengers per year (approx.)
Dulles International	Chantilly	15,600,000
Richmond International	Richmond	2,700,000
Norfolk International	Norfolk	2,800,000

Birthplace of an Ideal

> We hold these truths to be self-evident,
> that all men are created equal...
> — *Thomas Jefferson, Declaration of Independence*

All men are by nature free and independent, and have certain inherent natural rights . . . All power was originally lodged in and consequently is derived from the people.
— George Mason, 1776, whose ideas inspired Thomas Jefferson and James Madison, among others

Making a State

In 1776, while the Revolutionary War raged, Patrick Henry was elected Virginia's first governor under the state's first constitution. Twelve years later Virginia ratified the U.S. Constitution on June 25, 1788, becoming the tenth state. Virginia had at first refused to approve the Constitution because it did not have a bill of rights. In 1791 Congress adopted a Bill of Rights written by James Madison, who based it on the work of George Mason.

Virginia's state constitution was revised several times in the years to follow; the most recent revisions were in 1971. Perhaps the most significant revision was the 1902 constitution that took voting rights away from the majority of African-American Virginians. This constitution also made segregation legal. Further laws were passed to separate blacks from whites. African Americans had to use separate schools and hotels, and sit in separate railroad cars. Segregation remained a part of Virginia's history and culture until the 1960s.

Political History

Virginia has an impressive political pedigree when it comes to its history. The House of Burgesses, the first democratically elected legislative body in America, was formed in 1619. Now called the General Assembly, it is the oldest legislative body in the western hemisphere.

DID YOU KNOW?

Virginia has had three capitals in its long history. The first, Jamestown, was burned during Bacon's Rebellion in 1676. In 1699 British Governor Francis Nicholson then moved the capital to Williamsburg, where it remained until the Revolutionary War, when the capital moved to Richmond in 1780. During the Civil War Richmond was chosen as the Confederate capital.

Two early presidents from Virginia, Thomas Jefferson and James Madison, were champions of states' rights. They believed that the U.S. government's power should not extend beyond the specific outlines of the Constitution and that all other decisions should be left to state and local governments. Much of early U.S. politics had to do with this conflict over how much power should rest with the federal government. Today the argument continues, with the Republican Party pushing for less federal government involvement and the Democratic Party supporting more.

While Virginia has voted Republican in many presidential elections since 1948, Democrats have been the

▼ Thomas Jefferson modeled Virginia's first permanent capitol, in Richmond, after a Roman-era temple in France. In 1904 the capitol was renovated, and new wings were added. The west wing became the Senate chamber and the east wing the chamber for the House of Delegates.

Elected Posts in the Executive Branch

Office	Length of Term	Term Limits
Governor	4 years	Cannot serve two consecutive terms
Lieutenant Governor	4 years	None
Attorney General	4 years	None

dominant force in state politics. The General Assembly has remained mainly Democratic, although recent governors of Virginia have been Republicans. Arlington County, across the Potomac from the nation's capital, is one of the few areas in Virginia that has consistently voted Democratic in presidential elections.

▲ The Virginia legislature in session.

The Executive Branch

The executive branch of Virginia's state government includes three elected positions — governor, lieutenant governor, and attorney general. The governor's responsibilities include enforcing the laws of the state and preparing the state budget. Virginia governors have more powers than governors in many other states. The governor appoints most state officials, who are then confirmed by both houses of the General Assembly. The governor also has veto power over bills passed by the General Assembly.

The Legislative Branch

Virginia's legislative branch is the General Assembly. It is responsible for making and repealing laws, setting taxes, and approving expenditures of state money. The General Assembly is *bicameral*, which means it consists of two houses. The General Assembly meets in Richmond each January for thirty- or sixty-day sessions.

The Judicial Branch

Virginia's court system interprets laws and tries cases. The General Assembly selects the justices of the state supreme court and judges of the circuit courts. The supreme court justices serve twelve-year terms, while judges are elected for eight years and can be re-appointed by the General Assembly. The Virginia Court of Appeals, created in 1985, handles appeals from the lower courts, which include the thirty-one circuit courts, district courts, and juvenile and family courts.

> **DID YOU KNOW?**
>
> **S**ix First Ladies were born in Virginia: Martha Dandridge Custis Washington, Martha Wayles Skelton Jefferson, Letitia Christian Tyler, Ellen Lewis Herndon Arthur, Helen Herron Taft, and Edith Bolling Galt Wilson. Although Martha Jefferson and Ellen Arthur are counted among the U.S. First Ladies, both had died before their husbands were elected to the office of president.

General Assembly			
House	**Number of Members**	**Length of Term**	**Term Limits**
Senate	40 senators	4 years	None
House of Delegates	100 delegates	2 years	None

The White House via Virginia

Virginia has contributed more United States presidents than any other state.

GEORGE WASHINGTON (1789–1797)

Surveyor, soldier, and hero of the Revolution, Washington was unanimously elected first president of the United States. He is known as the "Father of His Country."

THOMAS JEFFERSON (1801–1809)

The third president of the United States, Jefferson drafted the Declaration of Independence and was a lawyer, musician, planter, and architect. He helped westward expansion with the Louisiana Purchase and support for the Lewis and Clark expedition. He also founded the University of Virginia.

JAMES MADISON (1809-1817)

The fourth president, James Madison, was known as the "Father of the Constitution" for his role in drafting the document. He served as U.S. secretary of state before he became president.

JAMES MONROE (1817–1825)

The fifth president, Monroe was a lawyer who served as a senator, United States Minister to France, governor of Virginia, and U.S. secretary of state and secretary of war, all before becoming president. He was the author of the Monroe Doctrine.

WILLIAM HENRY HARRISON (1841)

The ninth president, Harrison served the shortest term of any president. He caught a cold the day he entered office and died of pneumonia one month later.

JOHN TYLER (1841–1845)

The tenth president, Tyler served as governor of Virginia, U.S. senator, and vice president, and became president when William Henry Harrison died thirty days after his inauguration.

ZACHARY TAYLOR (1849–1850)

The twelfth president of the United States, Taylor was considered a military hero who won fame in the Mexican–American War before being elected. He died unexpectedly while in office.

WOODROW WILSON (1913–1921)

The twenty-eighth president, Wilson was a scholar and educator who served as president of Princeton University from 1902–1910 and was governor of New Jersey from 1911–1913. He led the country through World War I and was awarded the Nobel Peace Prize in 1919.

Local Politics

In 1870 the Virginia General Assembly passed a law that seemed strange to non-Virginians. The law decreed that any city with a population of five thousand or more would constitute a separate jurisdiction, fully independent of any county affiliation. That is why Virginia has both a Roanoke City and a Roanoke County.

Virginia, a Lot to Love

> ## Copacetic.
> — Bill "Bojangles" Robinson

I n describing their state, Virginians might use the word *copacetic,* a word supposedly coined by Virginia-born tap dance legend Bill "Bojangles" Robinson. It means "excellent."

In addition to its major role in American history, Virginia is also home to a number of cultural achievements.

▲ Ellen Glasgow

Literature

Master of the macabre, Edgar Allan Poe was raised and married in Richmond and gained national attention there on the staff of the *Southern Literary Messenger.* Although Poe is perhaps Virginia's most famous literary light, Virginia has produced several other prominent writers. In the 1930s Ellen Glasgow won a Pulitzer Prize for her novel about upper-class Virginia society, *In This Our Life.* Douglas Southall Freeman was awarded two Pulitzer Prizes, for his biography of Robert E. Lee in 1935 and for his

▼ Bill Robinson dances in the Shirley Temple film *The Little Colonel* (1934).

◀ Cast members of "The Waltons" at the opening of the Walton Mountain Museum. *From left to right the cast members are:* **Kami Cotler, Jon Walmsley, Judy Norton-Taylor, Mary McDonough, and Eric Scott.**

six-volume life of George Washington in 1958. Novelist Willa Cather (1876–1947) was born in Virginia but as a child was taken to Nebraska, the setting for her best-known novels about immigrant settlers in the Middle West, *O Pioneers!, The Song of the Lark,* and *My Antonia.* William Styron won the Pulitzer Prize for *The Confessions of Nat Turner* in 1967 and also wrote the best-selling *Sophie's Choice.*

Marguerite Henry wrote a famous children's novel about the ponies that live on the Eastern Shore, titled *Misty of Chincoteague* (1947). Another children's author, William Howard Armstrong, won the 1970 Newbery Medal for his novel *Sounder.*

Virginia writer Earl Hamner, Jr., is the creator of two successful and long-running television series, "The Waltons" and "Falcon Crest." Hamner based the fictional Walton family on his own. "The Waltons" was so popular that there is a Walton's Mountain Museum near Charlottesville, which recreates the locations from the Waltons's house in the television show.

The Arts

In 1932, during the Great Depression, Virginia actor Robert Porterfield founded the Barter Theater in Abingdon. He wanted to give unemployed actors a place to perform and theater-goers a chance to see shows. In Abingdon the people had food but no money, so at the Barter Theater they could exchange hams, vegetables, jellies, and apples for tickets.

Richmond's African-American Renaissance

▲ renaissance of African-American culture flourished in Richmond in the early- and mid-twentieth century. A section of Richmond called Jackson Ward served as a cradle of black culture, producing business leader Maggie Walker, the daughter of a former slave who became the first female bank president in America, as well as legendary "King of Tapology" Bill "Bojangles" Robinson, who danced with Shirley Temple in the film *The Little Colonel* (1935). The famous Hippodrome Theater on Jackson Ward's Second Street (called "The Deuce") fostered the talents of Duke Ellington, Billie Holiday, Ella Fitzgerald, Nat King Cole, and James Brown.

Playwrights received a Virginia ham in exchange for their works. In 1946 the Barter Theater became the State Theater of Virginia. It is the longest-running professional repertoire theater in the country.

OLD STONE HOUSE

◄ The curator at the Edgar Allan Poe Museum in Richmond.

The Richmond Ballet is the state's only professional dance troupe and one of the finest on the East Coast. Richmond is also home to the Richmond Symphony Orchestra, while Norfolk is home to the Virginia Symphony and the Virginia Opera.

Virginia has more than two hundred museums, including the Virginia Museum of Fine Arts in Richmond, the first state-supported art museum in the United States, and the Chrysler Museum in Norfolk, named one of the twenty best art museums in the country. It is most famous for its collection of decorative glass. Also in Norfolk is the

▼ Morris House at Washington and Lee University.

Hermitage Foundation Museum, which houses the largest private collection of Asian art in the United States. The Harrison Museum of African-American Culture in Roanoke showcases the achievements of African Americans, especially in western Virginia. Also in Roanoke is the Art Museum of Western Virginia, which displays the works of new artists from the Southern Appalachian region.

Education

Virginia has a proud history in higher education. The second oldest college in the United States was founded in Williamsburg in 1693 by King William III and Queen Mary II. The College of William and Mary (which severed its ties with Great Britain in 1776) has among its many distinguished graduates presidents Thomas Jefferson, James Monroe, and John Tyler.

Founded in 1749, Washington and Lee University in Lexington gets half its name from the nation's first president (who kept the school from bankruptcy in 1796). "Lee" was added in 1871 to honor Confederate General Robert E. Lee, the college's president from 1865 to 1870. It is now a small, private college with two thousand students drawn from the top-ranked high school students in the country. The United States's first state military college, Virginia Military Institute (VMI), was founded in Lexington in 1839. Confederate General "Stonewall" Jackson, considered one of the most brilliant minds in military history, was an instructor at VMI before the Civil War. In 1997 female cadets were admitted to the institute for the first time.

The oldest college for women in the South, Mary Baldwin College was founded in Staunton in 1842 as the Augusta Female Seminary. Hampton Normal and Agriculture Institute, founded after the Civil War for former slaves, has grown into Hampton University, the United States's foremost African-American university.

▲ The Virginia Military Institute in Lexington.

DID YOU KNOW?

The culture of Virginia's Powhatan Confederacy is preserved in the Pamunkey Indian Reservation Museum, and the nearby Mattaponi Reservation Museum has a necklace that belonged to Chief Powhatan's daughter, Pocahontas.

Educator and social thinker Booker T. Washington is a famous graduate.

Today the state's leading university is the University of Virginia, considered among the nation's best insitutions of higher learning. Thomas Jefferson founded the university in 1819, hoping to train the country's future leaders, and some of his buildings are still in use. Virginia Polytechnic Institute and State University (known as Virginia Tech, or Tech) in Blacksburg ranks among the top research institutions in the country. James Madison University in Harrisonburg, with twelve thousand students, is the largest public university in the state's Shenandoah region.

Sports

Virginians are enthusiastic followers of the state's many college and university football and basketball teams. Popular teams include the University of Virginia's Cavaliers football team, the University of Richmond's Spiders football and basketball teams, and Virginia Tech football heroes, the Hokies. Other NCAA Division 1 basketball teams with devoted fans are the College of William and Mary's Tribe, Hampton University's Pirates, James Madison University's Dukes, and Virginia Military Institute's Keyders.

Two of the best minor league teams in Virginia are the Richmond Braves, the top AAA farm team in the Atlanta Braves organization, which plays its home games at the Diamond, a 12,500-seat stadium, and the AAA Norfolk Tides, a farm team for the New York Mets that plays at the Harbor Park Stadium, one of the best minor league stadiums in the country. Mets superstars Dwight Gooden and Daryl Strawberry got their start with the Tides.

Competing in the East Coast Hockey League are the

Virtual Blacksburg

The town of Blacksburg, home to Virginia Tech, has an Internet counterpart of itself, Blacksburg Electronic Village (website: www.bev.net). The idea, which originated in Virginia Tech in the early 1990s, involved giving everyone in the community free Internet access and email, creating a model electronic "town within a town," where everything from shopping to a parent-teacher conference could be conducted on-line. Although there are critics of this techno-paradise, the consensus seems to be that Blacksburg is a tight-knit community of "very lucky nerds."

▼ Randolph-Macon Women's College, circa 1907.

Richmond Renegades, winners of the 1994–1995 Riley Cup Championship, and the Hampton Roads Admirals.

The Softball Hall of Fame in Petersburg is dedicated to the outstanding players of the professional United States Slo-Pitch Softball Association (USSSA). Richmond is home to the Round Robin Softball Tournament, one of the largest in the world. Every Memorial Day weekend more than four hundred teams from twenty states compete in parks around the city. The Virginia Sports Hall of Fame & Museum celebrates a century of local sports heroes.

▲ **Virginia Tech takes on Syracuse University.**

History-Making Virginians

And old Virginia with her noble stock.
— *Eugene Fitch Ware, poet*

Following are only a few of the thousands of people who lived, died, or spent most of their lives in Virginia and made extraordinary contributions to the state and the nation.

GEORGE MASON
STATESMAN

BORN: *December 1725, Fairfax County*
DIED: *October 7, 1792, Fairfax County*

One of the richest landowners in colonial Virginia, George Mason took an active role in local politics. He served in the House of Burgesses in 1759 and helped write the Virginia Constitution when the state broke away from English rule during the Revolutionary War. His writings on individual rights strongly impressed his neighbor Thomas Jefferson, who included Mason's ideas in the Declaration of Independence.

Mason was a fierce opponent of slavery who favored freeing slaves and educating them. He participated in the Constitutional Convention of 1787 in Philadelphia and voiced his opposition to the continuance of slavery at that time. He helped draft the document but refused to sign it until it included a bill of rights. The first ten amendments of the U.S. Constitution are based on the bill of rights he advocated. Mason spent his entire life in Virginia, where a university is named for him.

EDGAR ALLAN POE
WRITER

BORN: *January 19, 1809, Boston, MA*
DIED: *October 7, 1849, Baltimore, MD*

Orphaned by an actress mother when he was two years old, Poe was raised in Richmond by the Allan family. His foster father was a tobacco exporter. Poe attended the University of Virginia for one year, earning high marks in Latin and French. At eighteen he went to Boston and published his first volume of poems. From the age of twenty-two, his life was a continual struggle with poverty. For a few years he lived with his aunt, Maria Clemm, in Baltimore and fell in love with her daughter, Virginia, who was thirteen years younger than he was. All the while he wrote stories and sold them to journals in Baltimore and Philadelphia. He married his cousin Virginia in 1836 and moved to Philadelphia, where he wrote and published his most famous tales, including "The Tell-Tale Heart," "The Fall of the House of Usher," "The Cask of Amontillado," and "The Murders in the Rue Morgue," which is said to be the first detective story. He was also famous for his tales of terror, such as "The Black Cat" and "The Pit and the Pendulum." In 1844 Poe and his family moved to New York, where Virginia died of tuberculosis in 1847. After her death Poe was a broken man, suffering terrible bouts of depression and drinking heavily. He died in Baltimore of "acute congestion of the heart." His work continues to exert a tremendous influence on writers today.

BOOKER T. WASHINGTON
ACTIVIST

BORN: *April 5, 1856, Franklin County*
DIED: *November 14, 1915, Tuskegee, AL*

Born a slave in Franklin County in 1856, Washington always had a passion for learning. When he and his family were freed in 1865, they moved to West Virginia, where he woke up every day before dawn to work in salt and coal mines so that he would be free to attend school in the afternoons. At age sixteen he learned about the Hampton Normal and Agriculture Institute in Hampton, Virginia, a school dedicated to black education. He was admitted to the school, where he would be a teacher years later. In 1881 he became the organizer and president of the Tuskegee Institute in Alabama, where he established a reputation as a leading activist and social thinker who called for interracial cooperation. In 1901 he published his autobiography, *Up from Slavery*. He died in Tuskegee in 1915.

BILL "BOJANGLES" ROBINSON
TAP DANCER

BORN: *May 25, 1878, Richmond*
DIED: *November 1949, New York, NY*

First performing for nickels and dimes on street corners, Robinson, the grandson of a slave, became one of the world's foremost tap dancers. He was a vaudeville star and appeared in many major stage musicals. He broke into the movie business in the early 1930s and achieved his greatest fame and popularity in the four movies he made with Shirley Temple between 1935–1938. In 1989 Congress declared Robinson's birthday National Tap-Dancing Day.

RICHARD E. BYRD
EXPLORER

BORN: *October 25, 1888, Winchester*
DIED: *March 11, 1957, Boston, MA*

Born in Winchester, Richard Evelyn Byrd was a flying instructor for the U.S. Navy and, during World War I, made pioneering experiments of flying over water out of sight of land. In 1926 he and Floyd Bennett made what many consider to be the first flight over the North Pole. Later he was involved in six Antarctic expeditions, four of which were sponsored by the U.S. government.

ELLA FITZGERALD
JAZZ SINGER

BORN: *April 25, 1917, Newport News*
DIED: *June 15, 1996, Beverly Hills, CA*

Orphaned at the age of fifteen, Fitzgerald was placed in the Colored Orphan Asylum in Riverdale. She was later transferred to the New York Training School for Girls. She ran away from the school and was living on the streets of Harlem when, in 1934 at the age of sixteen, she made her singing debut at Harlem's Apollo Theater Amateur Night. She won first prize, and bandleader Chick Webb made her his orchestra's singer. Although she never received any formal vocal training, she had amazing technique and range and went on to achieve success in a six-decade-long career, making thousands of recordings and winning thirteen Grammy Awards. Fitzgerald became one of the most famous jazz singers in the world and remained an active performer until her death at the age of seventy-nine in 1996.

WILLIAM STYRON
WRITER

BORN: *June 11, 1925, Newport News*

After serving in the Marine Corps during World War II and graduating from Duke University in 1947, Styron published his first novel, *Lie Down in Darkness*, in 1951. His 1967 novel, *The Confessions of Nat Turner*, a fictional story of the 1831 Southhampton slave uprising, won the Pulitzer Prize but was criticized for exploiting slavery. African-American novelist James Baldwin defended Styron against charges of racism. Today the book is considered a classic. He is also the author of the critically acclaimed *Sophie's Choice* (1979), about a Holocaust survivor.

WARREN BEATTY
ACTOR AND DIRECTOR

BORN: *March 20, 1937, Richmond*

Henry Warren Beatty began acting as a child, as did his sister, actress Shirley MacLaine. He studied drama with famous acting teacher Stella Adler in 1959. He made his television debut that same year and made his film debut in *Splendor in the Grass* (1961). The film that made him a star was *Bonnie and Clyde*, a huge hit in 1967, which he also produced. In 1975 he wrote, produced, and starred in the movie *Shampoo* and made his directorial debut with 1978's *Heaven Can Wait*. In 1981 he was awarded an Oscar for Best Director for *Reds*, which he also produced. His 1998 comedy *Bulworth* was a political satire.

ARTHUR ASHE

ATHLETE AND ACTIVIST

BORN: *July 10, 1943, Richmond*
DIED: *February 6, 1993, New York, NY*

After graduating from high school, Ashe earned a tennis scholarship to the University of California at Los Angeles (UCLA). In 1963 he was chosen to represent the United States in the Davis Cup, becoming the first African American to play for the U.S. team. At UCLA he became known on a national level for his tennis ability, winning an individual and team National Collegiate Athletic Association (NCAA) Championship in 1965. He graduated in 1966 with a bachelor's degree in business administration.

In 1969, when he was the top-ranked U.S. player and one of the best tennis players in the world, Ashe applied for a visa to play in the South African Open, which was denied because of his skin color. He called for South Africa's expulsion from the tennis tour and the Davis Cup, and many supported his stance.

In 1975 he won the Wimbledon Championship and became the number one tennis player in the world. After retiring in 1980 Ashe worked as a journalist and television sports commentator and founded many charitable organizations. In 1988 Ashe learned that he was HIV positive, having contracted the disease from a blood transfusion. He started the Arthur Ashe Foundation for Defeat of AIDS (AAFDA) to raise awareness of the disease. Arthur Ashe died on February 6, 1993.

◀ Arthur Ashe playing at Wimbledon in 1975.

Virginia
History At-A-Glance

1859
Abolitionist extremist John Brown leads a failed raid on the U.S. Arsenal at Harper's Ferry and is hanged.

1765
Patrick Henry protests the Stamp Act.

1780
State capital moves to Richmond.

1619
First convention of the House of Burgesses in Jamestown; first Africans are brought to Virginia.

1676
Nathaniel Bacon's Rebellion drives British governor out of Jamestown.

1607
Jamestown established as first settlement of Virginia Colony.

1774
British governor John Murray dissolves the House of Burgesses; the first Virginia convention sends delegates to the Continental Congress.

1831
Nat Turner leads a slave rebellion.

1861
Civil War begins; Virginia secedes from the Union and coins the name Confederate States of America; Richmond becomes Confederate capital.

1612
John Rolfe begins cultivating tobacco for export.

1624
Virginia becomes a royal colony.

1699
Virginia's colonial government moves to Williamsburg.

1832
A bill to abolish slavery in Virginia loses by seven votes in the House of Delegates.

1600 — **1700** — **1800**

1492
Christopher Columbus comes to New World.

1607
Capt. John Smith and three ships land on Virginia coast and start first English settlement in New World — Jamestown.

1754–63
French and Indian War.

1773
Boston Tea Party.

1776
Declaration of Independence adopted July 4.

1777
Articles of Confederation adopted by Continental Congress.

1787
U.S. Constitution written.

1812–14
War of 1812.

United States
History At-A-Glance

1902
The poll tax in Virginia's revised constitution keeps African Americans from voting.

1976
Lawrence A. Davies and Noel C. Taylor are elected first black mayors of Virginia cities.

2001
On September 11, a hijacked airliner carrying 64 passengers and crew crashes into the Pentagon in Arlington, killing all onboard and 125 people at the Pentagon.

1870
Virginia readmitted to the Union.

1954
United States Supreme Court decides to end public school segregation; Virginia closes public schools to avoid compliance.

1970
Virginia's first Republican governor since 1886 elected.

1959
Virginia Supreme Court outlaws school closing; school integration begins.

1990
L. Douglas Wilder becomes the first elected black governor in the United States.

1900
"Jim Crow" segregation laws passed by legislature.

1971
Virginia's present-day state constitution is adopted.

1800	1900	2000

1848
Gold discovered in California draws 80,000 prospectors in the 1849 Gold Rush.

1869
Transcontinental Railroad completed.

1929
Stock market crash ushers in Great Depression.

1950–53
U.S. fights in the Korean War.

2000
George W. Bush wins the closest presidential election in history.

1917–1918
U.S. involvement in World War I.

1941–45
U.S. involvement in World War II.

1964–73
U.S. involvement in Vietnam War.

1861–65
Civil War.

2001
A terrorist attack in which four hijacked airliners crash into New York City's World Trade Center, the Pentagon, and farmland in western Pennsylvania leaves thousands dead or injured.

▼ A railroad station in Charlottesville, circa 1916.

Festivals and Fun For All

Check web site for exact date and directions.

Dog Mart, Fredericksburg

Dog Mart is a small festival with food, music, and a dog parade. Its history dates back to before the Revolution, when Native Americans used to come to the area to trade furs for the settlers' animals.

Hampton Jazz Festival, Hampton

The biggest names in jazz come to perform at Hampton Coliseum for the two-day festival in late June.
www.hampton.va.us/coliseum/jazz-updates.html

Virginia Highlands Festival, Abingdon

This two-week long festival starts in early August and is a showcase for Appalachian Mountain culture, featuring musicians, artists, writers, and crafts people. The area's largest craft show also features a hot-air balloon rally.
www.va-highlands-festival.org

Pony Swim and Auction, Chincoteague

The famous wild ponies of Chincoteague swim across the Assateague Channel on the last Wednesday in July and are auctioned off for $200.
www.chincoteague.net/ev-pony.html

International Azalea Festival, Norfolk

The festival, which takes place in the Norfolk Botanical Garden and celebrates Norfolk's importance to NATO, ends with an air show and the crowning of an Azalea Queen who reigns over a parade.
www.azaleafestival.org

Shenandoah Apple Blossom Festival, Winchester

First organized in 1924, the festival features five days of food, music, parades, a carnival, and the coronation of the Apple Blossom Queen. The festival usually occurs the first weekend in May.
www.apple-blossom.com

The Great American Duck Race, Winchester

Duck races are held on the second Saturday of August in Jim Barnett Park. There's also music and good food.

Old Time Fiddlers Convention and Fiddlefest, Galax

Galax is the world capital of old-time mountain music. In the second weekend of August, it is home to the oldest and largest mountain music convention in the world.
www.oldfiddlersconvention.com

Chincoteague Oyster Festival, Chincoteague

This oyster feast extravaganza features more oysters than you've ever seen in your life; held in early October.
www.chincoteague.net/ev-oyst.html

State Fair of Virginia, Richmond

For ten days in late September, Strawberry Hill Fairgrounds hosts rides, entertainment, agricultural exhibits, and flower shows.

www.statefair.com

Constitution Day Festival, Montpelier Estate, near Charlottesville

Held every year on September 17 at the beautiful home of President James Madison, who helped write the U.S. Constitution, this festival celebrates the composition of our government's central charter.

www.montpelier.org

Patrick Henry Speech Reenactment, St. John's Church, Richmond

St. John's was the site of Patrick Henry's famous "liberty or death" speech. A reenactment is performed annually on the closest Sunday to March 23.

www1.richmond.com/output.cfm?id=92243

James River Bateau Festival, Lynchburg

This festival celebrates the flat-bottomed boats, known as bateaux, used to transport tobacco in the late 1700s on Virginia waterways. The festival — a 120-mile (193-km) trek by bateau down the James River — runs for a week in mid-to-late September. All comers are encouraged to build their own bateau and join the waterborne parade.

www.batteau.org

Neptune Festival, Virginia Beach

Since 1974, on the last weekend in September, Virginia Beach has welcomed more than five hundred thousand visitors to bid farewell to summer. Events include a sand-sculpting competition, air shows, a surfing contest, live music, and a parade led by King Neptune himself and his royal court of tritons and princesses.

www.hrtide.com/partners/neptunefest

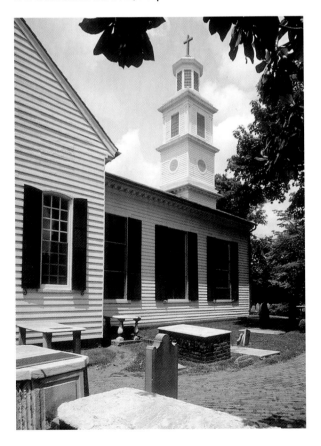

◄ St. John's Episcopal Church in Richmond.

Books

Arnold, James R. and Roberta Wiener. *On to Richmond: The Civil War in the East*. Minneapolis: Lerner Publications, 2001. This book is about the many Civil War battles that took place in Virginia and their importance to U.S. history.

Barrett, Tracy. *Virginia*. Tarrytown, NY: Benchmark Books, 1997. Learn more about Virginia past and present through history, photographs, and interviews with residents.

Bisson, Terry. *Nat Turner: Slave Revolt Leader*. New York: Chelsea House, 1988. This book recounts how Nat Turner led a rebellion against slavery in 1831.

Collier, Christopher and James Lincoln Collier. *The Paradox of Jamestown: 1585-1700*. Tarrytown, NY: Benchmark Books, 1998. Read about the first permanent English settlement in the United States and the tragic decision to permit slavery in the colony.

Severance, John. *Thomas Jefferson: Architect of Democracy*. New York: Clarion Books, 1998. Read about the life and ideas of this famous Virginian who helped write the U.S. Constitution and served as third president of the United States.

Web Sites

▶ All kinds of info
www.virginia.com/virginiaonline/allaboutva.htm

▶ Links to Virginia's cities' web sites
dir.yahoo.com/Regional/U_S__States/Virginia/Cities

▶ Commonwealth of Virginia homepage
www.state.va.us

▶ Web site of the Virginia Historical Society
www.vahistorical.org

▶ Alexandria's African-American history resource center
www.ci.alexandria.va.us/oha/bhrc

Note: Page numbers in *italics* refer to illustrations or photographs.